IN PURSUIT OF THE TRUTH

NIMMATHI NILAYAM

We dedicate this book for the glory of God...

Contents

Contents

Acknowledgements

We, at Nimmathi Nilayam, want to sincerely acknowledge the hardwork of a multitude of people. Yet, due to constraints & upon personal requests, names of no one is put up. This is both, to save privacy of the truth seekers, who worked diligently & unbiased, to search for the truth, presented in these pages & also to avoid speculations.

Our gratitude go on to our well wishers, friends, family members & supporters, around the globe & especially to the wonderful people, who worked hard to bring these documents under one book. Though small & precise, continuos efforts are being made to stick to the authenticty of all the nformation provided in these pages.

Our deepest thanks go to **God**, *the Real Truth*, without whose mercy & grace, none of these would ever exist.

About Us

We, at Nimmathi Nilayam, are a group of people, unseparated by the human inventions of divisions by caste, creed, race, sex & religion. We are geographically diverse & yet are connected to each other, thanks to the various online channels & social media.

We come from diverse educational backgrounds, that include doctors, engineers, lawyers, carpenters, farmers, professors, subject matter experts & also business owners. We identify ourselves under the name **Nimmathi Nilayam**, meaning **the House of Relief**.

Our aim is mainly to unite our fellow truth seekers under the banner of love, compassion & empathy. We, by no means, want to undermine an individual's personal faith or beliefs. We respect them to the utmost & encourage everyone to do the same. We believe, truth speaks for itself & there is no necessit for manipulation or coercion on anyone's part to propogate the truth, whatsoever.

We love you & respect your thoughts & beliefs. We are more than happy to have love grow amongst ourselves & reign within our hearts, for everone.

These pages are a work of deep seeking & we, at Nimmathi Nilaam, would urge eveyone to continue in the path of love, for **God is love & Love seeks good of all**.

Back to the Vedas

CHAPTER ONE

INTRODUCTION

- What we believe to be true, are they **really** the truth?
- Do we believe that they are true just because we were **taught** that they are the truth and we never looked any further?
- How do we really understand what the truth is?
- Are there any guidances or reliable sources which we can refer to, to know the reality?
- What is the purpose of our existence?

These are a few questions which come up in an inquisitive mind! Sadly, in this world which is filled with corruption, immorality, pride & wickedness, it is extremely hard to blindly trust any sources which pose to be true! This has ever been the state of mind of the people from time unmeasured, till today!

However, by testing every source, guidance & all sorts of means available, fortunately we can come to the conclusion of having a reliable source to begin our quest for truth - the **Holy Scriptures**! These were revealed to the humans as answers to their quest for the truth, found in the entity called "God".

All true seekers of God desire for the truth and welcome the truth that leads them to the Living, Loving, Almighty and the All-Powerful Creator. It is not just about religions or sects or faiths. Nor is it a mere collection of some facts, but it is the **driving force** behind all sincere seekers to the ultimate hope of experiencing God.

It is in this pursuit that men for ages have been looking towards nature, ancestors, heroes and even to unknown spirits for help. In the course of time, they had started worshiping them as well. It was this longing that resulted in the birth of the Vedas.

- Note: *The **Holy Bible** & the **Vedas** are the Scriptures which we would search, extensively...*

CHAPTER TWO

VEDAS: THE OUTLINE

Veda means *sacred scriptural knowledge*. This knowledge was obtained through dedication, devotion and meditation, by several hundred sages for years. These scriptures are divided into two parts:

- **Shruti** - *which is revealed*
- **Smriti** - *which is believed*

Shruti contains:

- **Vedas** - which give light or knowledge

Smriti contains:

- **Ithihasas** - parables like Mahabharata, Ramayana and Bhagvad Gita
- **Puranas** - short moral stories

These Ithihasas and Puranas, as perceived, were written at a later date to explain the morals of the Vedas.

There are few classes of Vedas. They are:

- **Samhitaas** or **Mantras** - *these contain a collection of chantings*
- **Aagamas** - *this contains commandments*
- **Bhramanas** - *this contains the meanings for Samhitaas*
- **Aranyakas** - *this contains meditations*
- **Upanishads** - *this contains philosophies*

Again, the Samhitaas are of four different types:

- **Rig Veda Samhitaa** - *a collection of hymns*
- **Yajur Veda Samhitaa** - *a collection of sacrificial formulas*
- **Sama Veda Samhitaa** - *a collection of songs*
- **Atharva Veda Samhitaa** - *a collection of spells and charms*

In an outline, Vedas start with the sinful nature of man and provide the remedy for getting out of this bondage of sin and show the way to the Creator God. Vedas, however, **do not** throw light on how man attained this sinful nature.

CHAPTER THREE

THE GODS IN THE VEDAS

Vedas begin with the worship of the gods of nature, namely:

- **Terrestrial gods** - Prithvi (earth), Agni (fire), Brahaspati (Jupiter) and Soma (plants)
- **Atmospheric gods** - Indra, Rudra, Maruts, Vayu, and Parjanya (storm, thunder and rain)
- **Celestial gods** - Dyaus (heaven), Varuna, Ushas & Asvins (twilight morning stars) and Surya, Mitra, Savitri, Ka, Vishnu (all associated with the sun).

As we have already seen, these gods were **the result of man's search** for the truth, which finally culminated in **Prajapati**, the Creator.

The 10th mandala of Rig Veda, chapter 121 & verse 10 says,

> "*Prajapati, the Lord of life, Lord of Creatures and Lord of Creations.*"

This understanding of the Creator, made man to cry to Him, as it is written in Bruhat Aranyaka Upanishad (1.3.28) saying,

> "***Asatoma sat gamaya,***

> ***Tamasoma jyotir gamaya,***
> ***Mruthyoma amrutham gamaya...***"

Which means, from untruth lead me to truth, from darkness lead me to light, from death lead me to eternal life.

CHAPTER FOUR

The Sinful Nature of Man

After having reached this stage of knowing the truth about crying to the Creator for help, the next step is obviously to follow the truth, which will ultimately help mankind to attain **Mukti** (Deliverance). It is at this stage, that man comes across the major hurdle, which is very well described in Prartha Snana Mantra,

> ***"Papokam, papa kanmokam, papathma papa samphava; thrahimam Pundarikaksha sarva papa hari hare..."***

Which means, I am born in sin, doer of sin, and a sinful self; I am the worst of all sinners, Lord save me from all my sins.

Why is sin a hurdle? Rig Veda 7.86.3 says,

> *"Because, it is an offense against God..."*

Sin has many names in Sanskrit Scriptures namely:

- ***pap*** - sin
- ***aag*** - fire
- ***dushkrit*** - evil deeds
- ***thamas*** - darkness
- ***prakrit*** - inborn nature
- ***asathya*** - untruth

Dr. S. Radhakrishnan said,

> "*we have sin with us from the beginning of history.*"

The Bruhat Aranyaka Upanishad says, that the ***Jeeva*** (soul) acquires evil, right at birth (4.3.8).

> "***Rog Sog Dhuk Paritab Bhandan Vyasnanicha, Aatma aparatha Vrukshanam phalarh edhani dehinam,***"

Which means, "what are the fruits of this sinful tree which is our body? Sickness, sorrow, pain, bondage and many other kinds of sins". No man is free from this bondage of sin.

CHAPTER FIVE

The Vedic way of Mukti: Deliverance

According to Bhagvad Gita, God does not accept karma either good or bad, as far as redemption of the soul is concerned (Bhagvad Gita 2:50).

Viveka Chudamani verse 147 says that,

> "*neither weapons, nor wind, nor fire, nor millions of deeds can remove this bondage. Only the wonderful sword of knowledge that comes out of discrimination sharpened by the grace of God can destroy it.*"

Again verse 6 says;

> "***Vadhanthu shastrani yadhanthu devane, Kurvanthu karmanibajanthu devata, Aatmaikayodena vinabpi mukitha, na chityathi bhramma shathanthrashpi.***"

Let them quote scriptures and sacrifice to gods; let them observe rituals and worship gods; but there is no liberation at all; no, not even in a hundred lifespans of Brahma put together, until the identity of one's self with the Divine Being is realized. Bhagvad Gita 11:53 says,

> "***Naham vedair na danena na ejyaya***
> ***sakya evamvidho drstavan asi mam yatha***"

Which means, neither by Vedic study, nor by austerities, nor by charities, nor by sacrifices can one behold Me. Nor by any works that you have done.

Regarding **Karma marga**'s rebirth cycle, the Poet Shiva Vakkiar says,

> "*Once milked, the same milk cannot enter into the breast. Once the butter is taken out of the milk, the same butter cannot mix with the same milk. Neither the flower that falls, can become a flower again. Then how can a man or woman be born in this world several times?*"

Regarding **Gnana marga**, the Vedas and Upanishads say, that we have to know the Purusha (for He is the knowledge) who has sacrificed His life for mankind.

> "***Gurureva paraa vidya***"

Which means, "God himself is the knowledge" This is a good verse to know.

Regarding **Yoga marga** or concentration of the mind, there is only one answer in the Vedas and Upanishads as to whom we should concentrate on. It is Purusha, the Almighty again. Mind concentration contains three important steps:

- ***Shravana*** - hearing about God from the Guru
- ***Manana*** - keeping on thinking about what we have heard
- ***Nididhyaasana*** - profound and repeated meditation on the word of God and dwelling in Him

Yoga simply means, "to unite with". Whom to unite with should be obvious. It is the Supreme Lord or Purusha. Shankara, the ancient sage admitted in Viveka Chudamani 3, that

> "*union with God is attained by the grace of God.*"

Also verse 56 says,

> "***Na yogena na sankhyena karmanano na vidhya Bhrahmathmaikkathva bodhena moksha; sidhyathey nanyatha,***"

Which means, neither by yoga, nor by knowing self, nor by karma, nor by learning, but by the realization of one's own identity with God, is liberation possible!

Bhakti marga (way of devotion), according to scholars, means spiritual love. The only God whom we can love is Purusha. If we can concentrate on this Purusha, then we will find Him and love Him as well. The Rig Veda says,

> "*"whom shall we worship other than Prajapati (Purusha)?"*"

Svetasvataara Upanishad (3.8) says,

> "*"By knowing Purusha, death is transcended. There is no other way".*"

CHAPTER SIX

MAN'S INVENTION TO GET RID OF THE BONDAGE OF SIN

Man, out of his own wisdom and knowledge, invented many ways to get rid of this bondage of sin. They are:

- ***Karma marga*** - way of works
- ***Gnana marga*** - way of knowledge
- ***Yoga marga*** - way of concentrating mind
- ***Bhakti marga*** - way of devotion

The word Karma means several things. They are:

- It may mean the deed or deeds of the individual human being. These deeds are:

1. ***Satvik*** - virtuous
2. ***Rajasik*** - pride
3. ***Tamasik*** - evil

These three are known ***Triguna*** or triple nature.

- It may mean the cycle of karma, ***karma samsara*** or ***karma chakra***.
- It may also mean ***karma yoga*** or ***nishkarma***, or a deed or deeds done without any desire for reward.

An individual's karma can be classified as follows:

- ***Sanchit karma*** - the accumulated deeds of all previous births, which get attached to the soul automatically at the time of each birth, in the rebirth cycle.
- ***Kriymana karma*** - good or bad deeds that the soul may further accumulate.
- ***Prarabdha karma*** - deeds which decide the destiny of the soul.

The main purpose of this rebirth cycle is, that the soul in each birth may reap the good or bad of all its karma of the past and present.

As per this doctrine, no one can ever know about his or her accumulated deeds, thereby not having any opportunity to correct his or her past, resulting in a hopeless uncertainty. In other words, karma is being stamped on the forehead of every human being, and the destiny of the soul is ceaselessly determined without the control of the individual. This had made Shri Shankaracharya to say in Bhajagovindam,

> ***"Punarapi janana punarapi marana; Punarapi janani jadarey sayana; Ih sansarey wah dustarey; Krupya parey pahi muararey,"***

Which means, repeated birth, repeated death, and repeated lying in mother's womb, is a difficult process to go through. Oh destroyer of death, save me by your grace.

CHAPTER SEVEN

ATONEMENT FOR SINS

Thertiriya Aranyaka verse 3 says,

"***Sarvapapa pariharo raktha prokshna mavasyam***"

Which means, that the redemption is through shedding of blood only. For this purpose God allowed mankind to sacrifice animals, in order to make them realize that there is a penalty for everyone's sins. Though the animal's blood is not a substitute, it was expected that man would repent and turn away from his sinful ways, by seeing the blood of the animal which is being shed on his behalf. But mankind started practicing it just as a ritual, and thus came into condemnation. If mankind were to be saved from this predicament, as Thertiriya Aranyaka 3rd verse says again,

"***...thad raktham Paranatmena punyadena baliyagam***"

Which means, that blood has to be through the sacrifice of God himself. The Purusha Sukta says, there is no other way other than the sacrifice of Purusha Prajapati.

"***Purushao vava yagna***"

Chandokya Upanishad 3.16.1. says,

"*God, the Purusha is the sacrifice.*"

Sama Veda Dandiya Mahabhramanam says,

"***Prajapathi devapyam aathmanam yagnam kruthva prayachita***"

Which means, God will offer himself as a sacrifice for the redemption of mankind. Sathpatha Bhramanam says,

"***Prajapathi yagnayaga***"

Which means, God Himself is the Sacrifice!

CHAPTER EIGHT

VEDAS ON THE SACRIFICIAL PURUSHA: THE REQUIREMENTS

The Rig Veda specifies ten important requirements for the sacrificial Purusha.

1. **Should be without a blemish (*Nishkalanka Purusha*):** Kaatyaayana Srautasootram describes in chapter 6, that water and fire were to be used for the purification of the animals, since blameless (defectless) animals are not available in this world.
2. **The Purusha has to be separated from others:** While sacrificing the horse, the sacrificial horse is always separated from other horses. A bush of thorns is usually placed on the head of the horse to inform the people that this horse is separated for the sacrifice. Also the head of the horse is considered to represent the Purusha (Sathapatha Brahmana 13th kanda, 6.2.2).
3. **The Purusha has to be rejected by his own people:** In Itareya Brahmana it is written that the sacrificial animal should be rejected by its father, mother, brother, sister and friends (2.16).

4. **The Yagna Purusha has to suffer silently:** Rig Veda 5.46.1 says, "Like a horse I have yoked myself, well knowing to the pole. I seek neither release nor turning back".
5. **The Purusha has to be tied to a post:** In Satapata Brahmana (III -7.3.1) it is written, never do they immolate an animal without tying it to a pole.

"***Na varute yapaat pasum alabhate kadachana.***"

It is important to tie the animal to a sacrificial pillar before it is sacrificed. This pillar is called ***Yupastampa*** (sacrificial pillar), which has now become a flag mast.

6. **The blood of the Sacrificial Man should be shed:** Bruhat Aranyaka Upanishad (3.9.28.2) says,

"***Tvacha evasya rudhiram, prasyandi tvacha utpatah, Tasmaattadarunnaat praiti, raso vrukshadi vahataat***"

As the sap comes of the cut tree, blood comes out of the Purusha who is cut.

7. **The sacrificed animal's bones should not be broken:** In Itareya Brahmana 2.6 it is stated that the sacrifice separates the twenty-six ribs of the animal without breaking them.
8. **The sacrificed Purusha should return to life:** The Bruhat Aranyaka Upanishad says,

"***Yad Vruksho vrukshano rohati, mulannavatharah punah, martyah svinmrutyuna vruknah, kasmaanmulaat prarohati, Retasa iti maavocata, jivatastat praja yate, dhanaruh a iva val crau vruksho, anjasaa pretya sammbhava***"

Which means, if the tree is cut, it will grow again from its root. But after the man (***martyah***) was cut off by death, from which root does he come forth? Do not say that he is from the ***ratas*** (seed or semen) because ***ratas*** comes from the one who lives. Remember this man is dead. But this man (Purusha) comes alive on his own.

9. **The flesh of the Purusha should be eaten by his saints:** In Satapata Brahmana (5.1.1.1,2) we find that Prajapati gave Himself up to them, thus the sacrifice became theirs, and indeed the sacrifice is the food of the gods (saints).
10. **The sacrifice is for all:** Verse 8 in Purusha Sukta explains,

> "***Tasmaad yagnatsarvahutah, pasuntamscakre voayaryaa, naananyaan gramyaasca ye.***"

By that sacrifice, all these originated: sprinkled ghee and all kinds of animals of the sky, forest and country. The significance of sprinkled ghee represents the original sacrifice. Verse 9 of Purusha Sukta says,

> "***Tasmaad yagnat sarvahuta, nucha samaari jagnire, Chandaamsi jagnine, tasmaad yajustas naada jaayatah.***"

From that sacrifice, Purusha offered everything that he had, including the Rig, Sama, Yajur Vedas and the Chandas (sacred writings).

CHAPTER NINE

VEDAS ON THE SACRIFICIAL PURUSHA: THE FULFILMENT

The fulfilment of the Vedic requirements of the ***Sacrificial Purusha*** is found in **Jesus Christ**!

1. **Jesus Christ was without any blemish:** In the Bible it is written,

> "*"Do not bring anything with a defect, because it will not be accepted on your behalf"* ***(Leviticus 22:20).***
>
> *"Whether male or female, present before the Lord an animal without defect"* ***(Leviticus 3:1).***
>
> *"In Him (Jesus Christ) there was no sin"* ***(1 John 3:5).***"

2. **Jesus Christ was separated from others:** The Bible says,

> "*"the soldiers platted a crown of thorns, and put it on his head, and they put on him a purple robe"* ***(John 19:2)***"

thus separating Him from others.

3. **Jesus Christ was rejected by his own people:** The Prophet Isaiah wrot

> "*"He (Jesus Christ) was despised and rejected and they shouted to crucify him".*"

Jesus said on the cross,

> "*"Eloi, Eloi, lama sabachthani", which means, "My God, My God, why have you forsaken me?" (**Matthew 27:46**).*"

4. **Jesus Christ suffered silently:**

> "*"He was oppressed and afflicted, yet He did not open his mouth. He was led like a lamb to the slaughter and as a sheep before the shearers is silent" (**Isaiah 53:7**).*"

5. **Jesus Christ was tied:Psalms 118:27** says,

> "*"bind the sacrifice with cords, even unto the horns of the altar".*"

6. **Jesus Christ's blood was shed:** This was fulfilled in Jesus Christ when he was nailed to the cross.

> "*"He did not enter by means of the blood of goats and calves; but entered the most holy place once for all by His own blood, having obtained eternal redemption. Without shedding of blood there is no redemption" (**Hebrews 9:12, 22**).*"

7. **Jesus Christ's bones were not broken:** In the Bible, **Exodus 12:46** says that the bones of the animal should not be broken. Six hours after the crucifixion,

> "*"when they (soldiers) came to Jesus, and saw that he was dead already, they broke not his legs"* ***(John 19:33).***"

8. **Jesus Christ rose again from the dead:**

> "*"Him (Jesus Christ) God raised up the third day, and showed him openly"* ***(Acts 10:40).***
>
> *"But now is Christ risen from the dead, and become the firstfruits of them that slept"* ***(1 Corinthians 15:20).***"

9. **Jesus Christ gave his body to be eaten:** At the last supper Jesus took the bread, gave thanks and gave it to his disciples saying,

> "*"Take and eat; this is my body. Then He took the cup, gave thanks, and offered it to them, saying, Drink from it, all of you. This is my blood of the new covenant, which is shed for many, for the forgiveness of sins"* ***(Matthew 26:26, 27).***"

10. **Jesus Christ was given to all:**

> "*"He who did not spare His own son, but gave him up for us all, how will he not also, along with him graciously give us all things?"* ***(Romans 8:32).***"

CHAPTER TEN

God's plan for Moksha: Eternal Life

For all have sinned, and come short of the glory of God. **Romans 3:23**

All we like sheep have gone astray; we have turned everyone to his own way; and the LORD has laid on him the iniquity of us all. **Isaiah 53:6**

For the wages of sin is death; but the gift of God is eternal life through Jesus Christ our Lord. **Romans 6:23**

And according to the law almost all things are purged with the blood, and without shedding of blood there is no remission. **Hebrews 9:22**

But God commended his love toward us, in that, while we were yet sinners, Christ died for us. **Romans 5:8**

For He has made him to be sin for us, who knew no sin; that we might be made the righteousness of God in him. **2 Corinthians 5:21**

The blood of Jesus Christ, His Son cleanses us from all sin. **1 John 1:7**

For God so loved the world that He gave His only begotten son, that whosoever believes in him should not perish, but have everlasting life. **John 3:16**

Herein is love, not that we loved God, but that he loved us, and sent His Son to be the propitiation for our sins. **1 John 4:10**

That if you shall confess with your mouth the Lord Jesus, and shall believe in your heart that God has raised him from the dead, you will be saved. **Romans 10:9**

Or do you underestimate His wealth of kindness and tolerance and enduring patience, unmindful that God's kindness is meant to lead you toward repentance? But in line with your obstinacy and impenitence of heart you are treasuring up for yourself anger for the day of anger and the revealing of the righteous judgment of God, who will reward each person according to his deeds. **Romans 2:4 - 6**

For there is no partiality with God. **Romans 2:11**

Neither is there salvation in any other: for there is none other name under heaven given among men, whereby we must be saved. **Acts 4:12**

So today if you hear His voice, harden not your heart, but come boldly unto the throne of grace, that you may obtain mercy, pardon and ETERNAL LIFE (***Moksha***).

Come unto Me, all ye that labour and are heavy laden, and I will give you rest. **Matthew 11:28**

Behold, I stand at the door, and knock; if any man hear my voice, and open the door, I will come in to him, and will sup with him, and he with Me. **Revelation 3:20**

I am the way, the truth and life; no one comes to the Father except through Me. **John 14:6**

Verily, verily, I say unto you, he that hears My word, and believes in Him that sent Me, has everlasting life, and shall not come into condemnation; but is passed from death unto life. **John 5:24**

For what shall it profit a man, if he shall gain the whole world, and lose his own soul? **Mark 8:36**

CHAPTER ELEVEN

MORE VEDIC REFERENCES TO JESUS

Sahasranamavali acknowledges Jesus Christ in the following praises:

- ***Om Shri Brahmaputraya namaha:*** O Lord, The Son of God, we praise you.
- ***Om Shri Umathyaya namaha:*** O Lord, who is born of the Spirit, we praise you.
- ***Om Shri Kanni Sudhaya namaha:*** O Lord, who is born of a virgin, we praise you.
- ***Om Shri Daridra Narayanaya namaha:*** O Lord, who became poor for our sake, we praise you.
- ***Om Shri Vidhiristaya namaha:*** O Lord, who is circumcised, we praise you.
- ***Om Shri Panchagayaya namaha:*** O Lord, who bore five wounds on your body, we praise you.
- ***Om Shri Vruksha-shul Aruthaya namaha:*** O Lord, who offered yourself as a sacrifice on a trishool like tree (three headed spear), we praise you.
- ***Om Shri Mruthyanjaya namaha:*** O Lord, who got victory over death, we praise you.

- ***Om Shri Shibilistaya namaha:*** O Lord, who willingly offered your flesh to be eaten by your saints, we praise you.
- ***Om Shri Thatchina Moorthyaya namaha:*** O Lord, who is seated by the side of the Father, we praise you.
- ***Om Shri Mahadevayaya namaha:*** O Lord, who is Lord of lords, we praise you.

Bhavishya Mahapurana, book 3, chapter 2, verse 34 says,

> ***"Ko bhavaanithi tham praaha Sobhovaachamudaanwitha: Eshaputhram cha maam vidhi Kumaaree garbha sambahavam Aham Eesa Maseeha nama:"***

Which means, (king Saka asks) "May I know who you are? That man replied happily, I am the Son of God, born to a virgin. My name is Jesus Christ (Eesa Maseeha)".

CHAPTER TWELVE

ADOPTED CULTURAL AND THEOLOGICAL IDENTITIES OUTSIDE THE VEDAS

Following are a few practices adopted culturally, from the Bible, which find no roots in the Vedas:

- The festival of Shivaratri is celebrated by keeping a vigil throughout that night to thank god who had saved a hunter, who lost his way in the jungle. However, nowhere does the Vedic account record this practice and instruction.

The Bible says that the Lord kept a vigil on the day of Passover and delivered the people of Israel from Egypt. In remembrance of this day and to honour the Lord, the Israelites in turn keep a vigil on this night every year.

- On this day of Passover, God instructed Moses to mark the main doors of their houses and the top and two side posts with the blood of the lamb, which was to be sacrificed by each family, as a mark of identification for the purpose of protection.

These same markings with the red powder (vermillion) can be seen in majority of the Indian houses, even today. Vedas, however, do not instruct this.

- While on a journey, Jacob slept for the night by keeping a stone as a pillow and dreamt, seeing angels of God ascending and descending on a ladder set between earth and heaven, and the Lord stood above it. Next morning he took the stone, and set it up as a pillar, and poured oil over it, and he named that place as Bethel (house of God).

In India also, one can see the stone with oil, which has become "Shivalinga". Swami Vivekananda once said that he found it a mystery as there was no record whatsoever of its origin.

- In the Bible, God told Moses to bring a red heifer without spot and kill it as a sacrifice for the Lord. Her skin, her flesh, blood and dung shall be burnt. A clean man shall gather up the ashes of the heifer and keep it in the holy place. This ash will be mixed with water and will be sprinkled on the body of the people, for the purpose of purification from their sins (**Numbers 19:1 - 9**).

During the Vedic period, three different kinds of sacrifices were in practice:

1. ***Nara medhya yagna*** - Human body sacrifice
2. ***Go medhya yagna*** - Cow sacrifice
3. ***Ashwa medhya yagna*** - Horse sacrifice

For ***Go medhya yagna***, the cow should be a red one. Even today, if a Brahmin wants to do some ceremonial duty in his house, he will look for a red cow and perform ***pooja*** before it. The sacrificial cow has now become a sacred cow, because cow is no longer sacrificed by law. Therefore, people burn only the cow's dung and they collect these ashes and mix it with water and apply it on their body or generally on their forehead as ***Vibhooti***. However the practice of using ashes is not instructed anywhere in the Vedas.

- Since the sacrificed cow was to be positioned upside down on the altar before burning, a long three headed fork like tool was used. In addition, to collect and store these ashes, several types of vessels were used. In the Bible the Lord told, "you shall make its pans to receive its ashes, and its shovels and its basins and its forks and its fire pans; you shall make all its utensils of bronze" **(Exodus 27:3)**.

Similarly in the Indian temples also, all these vessels are made out of bronze. Ever since the sacrifices have been stopped, the meat fork with three-headed spear is kept near the altar in front of the temple. This has now become ***Trishool***.

- In the Bible, the priest, while he is inside the holy of the holiest part of the temple, should make a sound with the bells, as well as while coming out of it. He should have his undergarments from the waist to the knee. The sacrificial animal should have a small string, bearing the name of the family. The priest should mention the name of the family and then sacrifice. He should wear an engraved plate on his turban saying, "Holy to the Lord" **(Exodus 28:34 - 37, 42)**.

In the Indian temples also, when the priest goes inside the holy of the holiest place for prayer, he makes the noise of the bell and comes out with the noise of the bell. He wears a piece of cloth from his hip to the knee over his clothing. When the people bring their offerings to God, he always asks them on whose name should it be offered?

- In the Bible, Moses was given instructions and blueprints of building the Tabernacle - the dwelling place for God. This is sometimes termed as the Sanctuary. Bible specifically provides the measurements dimensions of the structure, that includes the Courtyard, the Holy Place & the Most Holy Place.

Most of the temples that we see today, have a similar structure - the outer court that has sacrificial arrangements, an outer room for everyone to gather & the inner room, where the idol of the deity is placed. This blueprint is not found anywhere in the Vedic literature.

- Learning of the Sanctuary from the Bible, we find that the entrance to the Santuary had one gateway. This gateway was specifically instructed to be built, facing the East. The theological explanation to this was that the Israelites had forgotten their Creator & started worshipping the sun as a deity. They adopted this practice, from their neighbouring clans. To make the Israelites realize of the true living God, the instruction was made to build the gateway, facing the east direction, so that whoever would enter the Sanctuary, had to tun back towards the east, the direction where the sun rises & come back to God. This was an oject lesson for the Israelites.

In today's Vaastu science, houses facing the east are considered the most compliant & auspicious houses. However, there is no reason to this belief. The roots are not even present in the Vedas.

CHAPTER THIRTEEN

VEDAS POINT TO THE HOLY BIBLE

Here, in the following, we see the close similarities of the Vedas with the Bible.

As the Bible says, that

> "*"God is a Spirit, and they that worship him must worship him in spirit and in truth"* ***(John 4:24).***"

The Yajur Veda (32:3) also says,

> "***Nathasya prathima asityasya nammahastha***"

Which means, God has no image and His name is Holy.

> "**Vagya vai Brahmma** - *the word is Brahmma (Creator), Bruhat Aranyaka Upanishad*
>
> **Shabdo vai Brahmma** - *the voice is Brahmma. Brahmmavindu Upanishad*
>
> **Shabdaksharam Param Brahmma** - *the voice and word became absolute God.*"

The Bible says,

> "*"In the beginning was the Word, and the Word was with God, and the Word was God ... and the Word was made flesh (Jesus)"* ***(John 1:1, 14).***"

As seen earlier, the Vedas start with the sinful nature of man and provide the remedy for getting out of this bondage of sin and show the way to the Creator God. Vedas, however, do not throw light on how man attained this sinful nature.

It is here that the Holy Bible provides us information both prior to Man's fall & beyond the Redemption of humanity, as seen below:

> "*In the beginning God created the heaven and the earth.* ***(Genesis 1:1)***"

> "*And he said, Who told thee that thou wast naked? Hast thou eaten of the tree, whereof I commanded thee that thou shouldest not eat? And the man said, The woman whom thou gavest to bewith me, she gave me of the tree, and I did eat.* ***(Genesis 3:11, 12)***"

> "*Wherefore, as by one man sin entered into the world, and death by sin; and so death passed upon all men, for that all have sinned: For if by one man's offence death reigned by one; much more they which receive abundance of grace and of the gift of righteousness shall reign in life by one,* ***Jesus Christ****. For as by one man's disobedience many were made sinners, so by the obedience of one shall many be made righteous. That as sin hath reigned unto death, even so might grace reign through righteousness unto eternal life by* ***Jesus Christ*** *our Lord.* ***(Romans 5:12, 17, 19, 21)***"

> "*Even when we were dead in sins, hath* ***quickened*** *us together with Christ, (by grace ye are saved;) And hath raised us up together, and* ***made us sit together in heavenly places in Christ Jesus****: That in the ages to come he might*

> *shew the exceeding riches of his grace in his kindness toward us through Christ Jesus.* ***(Ephesians 2:5 - 7)***"

As we see from the verses above that the Holy Bible records information about ***Creation, Fall of humanity, Redemption*** & ***Eternity***, we can most assuredly trust the account of the Holy Bible, because we witnessed that the Vedas pointed to the same story, in part.

The Ten Commandments

CHAPTER FOURTEEN

PRE-WORDS

The Ten Commandments, also known as the ***Decalogue***, are a set of commandments which the Holy Bible describes as been given by God to the whole humanity. The Ten Commandments are listed numerously throughout the Holy Bible.

Though also known as the **Law**, it is seen that there is a stunning resemblance between the Law and the very Character of God. These are listed below:

"*God is Spiritual.* ***John 4:24***
His Law is Spiritual. ***Romans 7:14***"

"*God is Love.* ***1 John 4:8, 16***
His Law is Love. ***Matthew 22:37 - 40***"

"*God is Truth.* ***John 14:6***
His Law is Truth. ***Psalm 119:142***"

"*God is Righteous.* ***1 Corinthians 1:30***
His Law is Righteous. ***Psalm 119:172***"

"*God is Holy.* ***Isaiah 6:3***
His Law is Holy. ***Romans 7:12***"

"*God is Perfect.* ***Matthew 5:48***

His Law is Perfect. ***Psalm 19:7***"

"*God stands Forever.* ***James 1:17***
His Law stands Forever. ***Psalm 111:7, 8***"

"*God is Good.* ***Luke 18:19***
His Law is Good. ***Romans 7:12***"

"*God is Just.* ***Deuteronomy 32:4***
His Law is Just. ***Romans 7:12***"

"*God is Pure.* ***1 John 3:3***
His Law is Pure. ***Psalm 19:8***"

"*God is Unchangeable.* ***James 1:17***
His Law is Unchangeable. ***Matthew 5:18***"

We can thus conclude that the Law is **reflection of God's Character**. It is similar to the **mirror image** of anyone, who views a mirror!

> "*And God said, Let us make man in* ***our image****, after our likeness: and let them have dominion over the fish of the sea, and over the fowl of the air, and over the cattle, and over all the earth, and over every creeping thing that creepeth upon the earth. So* ***God created man in his own image****, in the image of God created he him; male and female created he them.*
>
> ***Genesis 1:26, 27***"

> "*Even every one that is called by my name: for* ***I have created him for my glory****, I have formed him; yea, I have made him.*
>
> ***Isaiah 43:7***"

"*And he said, I beseech thee, shew me thy glory. And he said,* ***I will make all my goodness pass before thee****, and* ***I will proclaim the name of the LORD*** *before thee; and* ***will begracious*** *to whom I will be* ***gracious****, and* ***will shew mercy*** *on whom I will shew mercy.*

Exodus 33:18, 19"

Thus, from the above verses, we can conclude the following:

- Law is reflection or image of God's Character.
- Man was created in God's image.
- Man was created for God's glory.
- Glory of God is His Character.
- Hence, Man's life was supposed to be the Ten Commandments in action.

Let us now look into each of the Commandments and understand **God's Nature** through them. For this, we will look into the Holy Bible and the Vedas (some commandments are mentioned) and draw out a clearer understanding about Him.

CHAPTER FIFTEEN

THE FIRST COMMANDMENT

No one and nothing before God

The Holy Bible

"*I am the LORD thy God, which have brought thee out of the land of Egypt, out of the house of bondage. Thou shalt have no other gods before me.*

Exodus 20:2, 3"

"*I am the LORD thy God, which brought thee out of the land of Egypt, from the house of bondage. Thou shalt have none other gods before me.*

Deuteronomy 5:6, 7"

"*Then saith Jesus unto him, Get thee hence, Satan: for it is written, Thou shalt worship the Lord thy God, and him only shalt thou serve.*

Matthew 4:10"

"*And Jesus answered and said unto him, Get thee behind me, Satan: for it is written, Thou shalt worship the Lord thy God, and him only shalt thou serve.*

Luke 4:8"

"*No man can serve two masters: for either he will hate the one, and love the other; or else he will hold to the one, and despise the other. Ye cannot serve God and mammon.*

Matthew 6:24"

The Vedas

"*Prajapati, the Lord of life, Lord of Creatures and Lord of Creations.*

Rig Veda, Mandala 10, Chapter 121, Verse 10"

Regarding the Gnana marga, which was a way devised by humans to attain salvation, the Vedas and Upanishads say, that we have to know the Purusha (for He is the knowledge) who has sacrificed His life for mankind.

"*Gurureva paraa vidya.*"

which means, "God himself is the knowledge".

"*Na yogena na sankhyena karmanano na vidhya;*

Bhrahmathmaikkathva bodhena moksha; sidhyathey nanyatha,

Viveka Chudamani 56,"

which means, neither by yoga, nor by knowing self, nor by karma, nor by learning, but by the realization of one's own identity with God, is liberation possible!

"*Whom shall we worship other than Prajapati (Purusha)?*
Rig Veda"

"*By knowing Purusha, death is transcended. There is no other way.*
Svetasvataara Upanishad 3:8"

Conclusion

The Almighty God is the Creator Himself. There are no other gods beside Him. Vedas teach that most of the gods (terrestrial, atmospheric & celestial gods) are an imagination of humans to get rid of sin and to fulfil their own desires. Please refer to the first section - ***Back to the Vedas***, for this information.

How great is the Almighty God, in front of Whom everything else loses its significance! Everything which exists is because He brought them into existence. There is no beginning and no end to Him. He is Eternity. Our worship should only be for Him, the Almighty God, Who has created everything and has the power to redeem everything, as there is no one else who owns the Creation, but He Himself, being the Creator!

This Great God, though being Almighty, cares so much for us, who are nothing in front of Him! His love is manifested to us as we read,

"*For God so loved the world, that he gave his only begotten Son, that whosoever believeth in him should not perish, but have everlasting life. For God sent not his Son into the world to condemn the world; but that the world through him might be saved.*
John 3:16, 17"

The First Commandment calls us to worship God, the Creator, Whom both the Holy Bible (Christ) and the Vedas (Purusha) point to as solely being worthy for receiving our worship.

CHAPTER SIXTEEN

The Second Commandment

Idolatry

The Holy Bible

"Thou shalt not make unto thee any graven image, or any likeness of any thing that is in heaven above, or that is in the earth beneath, or that is in the water under the earth: Thou shalt not bow down thyself to them, nor serve them: for I the LORD thy God am a jealous God, visiting the iniquity of the fathers upon the children unto the third and fourth generation of them that hate me; And shewing mercy unto thousands of them that love me, and keep my commandments.

Exodus 20:4 - 6"

"Thou shalt not make thee any graven image, or any likeness of any thing that is in heaven above, or that is in the earth beneath, or that is in the waters beneath the earth: Thou shalt not bow down thyself unto them, nor serve

them: for I the LORD thy God am a jealous God, visiting the iniquity of the fathers upon the children unto the third and fourth generation of them that hate me, And shewing mercy unto thousands of them that love me and keep my commandments.

Deuteronomy 5:8 - 10"

"*Turn ye not unto idols, nor make to yourselves molten gods: I am the LORD your God.*

Leviticus 19:4"

"*Ye shall make you no idols nor graven image, neither rear you up a standing image, neither shall ye set up any image of stone in your land, to bow down unto it: for I am the LORD your God.*

Leviticus 26:1"

"*Thou shalt make thee no molten gods.*

Exodus 34:17"

"*Take ye therefore good heed unto yourselves; for ye saw no manner of similitude on the day that the LORD spake unto you in Horeb out of the midst of the fire: Lest ye corrupt yourselves, and make you a graven image, the similitude of any figure, the likeness of male or female, The likeness of any beast that is on the earth, the likeness of any winged fowl that flieth in the air, The likeness of any thing that creepeth on the ground, the likeness of any fish that is in the waters beneath the earth: And lest thou lift up thine eyes unto heaven, and when thou seest the sun, and the moon, and the stars, even all the host of heaven, shouldest be driven to worship them, and serve them, which the LORD thy God hath divided unto all nations under the whole heaven.*

Deuteronomy 4:15 - 18"

"*Cursed be the man that maketh any graven or molten image, an abomination unto the LORD, the work of the hands of the craftsman, and putteth it in a secret place. And all the people shall answer and say, Amen.*

Deuteronomy 27:15"

"*And the LORD passed by before him, and proclaimed, The LORD, The LORD God, merciful and gracious, longsuffering, and abundant in goodness and truth, Keeping mercy for thousands, forgiving iniquity and transgression and sin, and that will by no means clear the guilty; visiting the iniquity of the fathers upon the children, and upon the children's children, unto the third and to the fourth generation.*

Exodus 34:6, 7"

"*The LORD is longsuffering, and of great mercy, forgiving iniquity and transgression, and by no means clearing the guilty, visiting the iniquity of the fathers upon the children unto the third and fourth generation.*

Numbers 14:18"

"*Know therefore that the LORD thy God, he is God, the faithful God, which keepeth covenant and mercy with them that love him and keep his commandments to a thousand generations; And repayeth them that hate him to their face, to destroy them: he will not be slack to him that hateth him, he will repay him to his face.*

Deuteronomy 7:9, 10"

"*I am the LORD: that is my name: and my glory will I not give to another, neither my praise to graven images.*

Isaiah 42:8"

"*But that we write unto them, that they abstain from pollutions of idols, and from fornication, and from things strangled, and from blood.*

Acts 15:20"

"*Forasmuch then as we are the offspring of God, we ought not to think that the Godhead is like unto gold, or silver, or stone, graven by art and man's device. And the times of this ignorance God winked at; but now commandeth all men every where to repent:*

Acts 17:29, 30"

"*But now I have written unto you not to keep company, if any man that is called a brother be a fornicator, or covetous, or an idolater, or a railer, or a drunkard, or an extortioner; with such an one no not to eat.*

1 Corinthians 5:11"

"*Know ye not that the unrighteous shall not inherit the kingdom of God? Be not deceived: neither fornicators, nor idolaters, nor adulterers, nor effeminate, nor abusers of themselves with mankind, Nor thieves, nor covetous, nor drunkards, nor revilers, nor extortioners, shall inherit the kingdom of God.*

1 Corinthians 6:9, 10"

"*Neither be ye idolaters, as were some of them; as it is written, The people sat down to eat and drink, and rose up to play.*

1 Corinthians 10:7"

"*Wherefore, my dearly beloved, flee from idolatry.*

1 Corinthians 10:14"

> "*Ye know that ye were Gentiles, carried away unto these dumb idols, even as ye were led.*
> **1 Corinthians 12:2**"

> "*And what agreement hath the temple of God with idols? for ye are the temple of the living God; as God hath said, I will dwell in them, and walk in them; and I will be their God, and they shall be my people.*
> **2 Corinthians 6:16**"

> "*Now the works of the flesh are manifest, which are these; Adultery, fornication, uncleanness, lasciviousness, Idolatry, witchcraft, hatred, variance, emulations, wrath, strife, seditions, heresies, Envyings, murders, drunkenness, revellings, and such like: of the which I tell you before, as I have also told you in time past, that they which do such things shall not inherit the kingdom of God.*
> **Galatians 5:19 - 21**"

> "*For this ye know, that no whoremonger, nor unclean person, nor covetous man, who is an idolater, hath any inheritance in the kingdom of Christ and of God.*
> **Ephesians 5:5**."

This verse and the next both show the connection between covetousness and idolatry - when you covet something, it becomes your idol, and therefore your god (breaking the 1st commandment also).

> "*Mortify therefore your members which are upon the earth; fornication, uncleanness, inordinate affection, evil concupiscence, and covetousness, which is idolatry:*
> **Colossians 3:5**"

"*For they themselves shew of us what manner of entering in we had unto you, and how ye turned to God from idols to serve the living and true God;*
1 Thessalonians 1:9"

"*Little children, keep yourselves from idols. Amen.*
1 John 5:21"

"*And the rest of the men which were not killed by these plagues yet repented not of the works of their hands, that they should not worship devils, and idols of gold, and silver, and brass, and stone, and of wood: which neither can see, nor hear, nor walk:*
Revelation 9:20"

"*But the fearful, and unbelieving, and the abominable, and murderers, and whoremongers, and sorcerers, and idolaters, and all liars, shall have their part in the lake which burneth with fire and brimstone: which is the second death.*
Revelation 21:8"

"*Blessed are they that do his commandments, that they may have right to the tree of life, and may enter in through the gates into the city. For without are dogs, and sorcerers, and whoremongers, and murderers, and idolaters, and whosoever loveth and maketh a lie.*
Revelation 22:14, 15"

The Vedas

"*Vadhanthu shastrani yadhanthu devane, Kurvanthu karmanibajanthu devata,*

Aatmaikayodena vinabpi mukitha, na chityathi bhramma shathanthrashpi.
Viveka Chudamani 6."

Let them quote scriptures and sacrifice to gods; let them observe rituals and worship gods; but there is no liberation at all; no, not even in a hundred lifespans of Brahma put together, until the identity of one's self with the Divine Being is realized.

"*Naham vedair na danena na ejyaya sakya evamvidho drstavan asi mam yatha*
Bhagvad Gita 11:53,"

which means, neither by Vedic study, nor by austerities, nor by charities, nor by sacrifices can one behold Me. Nor by any works that you have done.

"*andham tamaḥ pravisanti ye 'sambhutim upasate tato bhuya iva te tamo ya u sambhutyam rataḥ*
Isha Upanishad 9, Shukla Yajur Veda 40."

"*Endowed with such a faith, he endeavours to worship a particular demigod and obtains his desires. But in actuality these benefits are bestowed by Me alone. The demigods cannot award benedictions to their devotees without the permission of the Supreme Lord. The less intelligent living entity does not know this, and therefore he foolishly goes to the demigods for some benefit. But the pure devotee, when in need of something, pray only to the Supreme Lord. A living entity goes to the demigods usually because he is mad to fulfil his lust [for material things]. Devotional service to the Supreme Lord and the worship of a demigod cannot be on the same platform, because worship of a demigod is material and devotional service to the Supreme Lord is completely spiritual. Men of small intelligence worship the demigods, and their fruits are limited and temporary. Those who worship the demigods go to the planets of the demigods, but My devotees ultimately reach My supreme planet.*

Bhagvad Gita 7:22"

"*Some commentators on the Bhagvad Gita say that one who worships a demigod can reach the Supreme Lord, but here it is clearly stated that the worshipers of demigods go to the different planetary systems where various demigods are situated, just as a worshiper of the sun achieves the sun or a worshiper of the demigod of the moon achieves the moon. It is not that everyone, regardless of whatever demigod is worshipped, will reach the Supreme Personality of Godhead. That is denied here, for it is clearly stated that the worshipers of demigods go to different planets in the material world but the devotee of the Supreme Lord goes directly to the supreme planet of the Personality of Godhead.*

Bhagvad Gita 7:23"

"*The ignorant believe that un-manifest Para Brahma (One God) incarnates or takes manifestations, because they do not completely understand My highest, immutable, incomparable, and transcendental existence.*

Bhagvad Gita 7:24"

"*All those who do idol worship, All those who worship demigods are materialistic people.*

Bhagvad Gita 7:19 - 21"

"*Of that God you cannot make any images.*

Yajur Veda 3:32"

"*God is formless and bodiless.*

Yajur Veda 32:3"

Conclusion

Both the Holy Bible and the Vedas declare that God is endless and cannot be shaped into a finite thing or into any form. The process of making idols and graven images are thus condemned and discouraged in the Holy Scriptures.

The Scriptures encourage us to worship God through faith. When a person makes a graven image or any form, he limits his faith and **creates** his god from the things **created by the Almighty God**! This most likely becomes an insult to the One who created everything! This makes the person to seem to be like "creator of his Creator"! It is incoherent to even visualize such a pride! Hence the Holy Scriptures forbid us to do such.

On the other hand, this Commandment shows us the very Character of God - Endless, Infinite & Almighty! A duplicate or a clone of such an entity cannot be reproduced or recreated, whatsoever.

The Holy Bible goes on to magnify this Commandment saying that anything which comes between God and us, in our lives, becomes an idol for us and is a stumbling block for us to reach God. It might be anything which is very dear to us - our families, our friends, our loved items, our jobs, any food item, any unnecessary pleasure etc. These can never take the position of God, as these are just mere gifts which God has given us, out of His love.

The Second Commandment, thus calls us to focus much deeply towards God and encourages us to go away from any distractions or stumbling blocks which stop us to reach God.

CHAPTER SEVENTEEN

THE THIRD COMMANDMENT

Vain use of God's Name

The Holy Bible

"*Thou shalt not take the name of the LORD thy God in vain; for the LORD will not hold him guiltless that taketh his name in vain.*

Exodus 20:7"

"*Thou shalt not take the name of the LORD thy God in vain: for the LORD will not hold him guiltless that taketh his name in vain.*

Deuteronomy 5:11"

"*And ye shall not swear by my name falsely, neither shalt thou profane the name of thy God: I am the LORD.*

Leviticus 19:12"

“*I am the LORD: that is my name: and my glory will I not give to another, neither my praise to graven images.*

Isaiah 42:8”

“*After this manner therefore pray ye: Our Father which art in heaven, Hallowed be thy name.*

Matthew 6:9”

“*And he said unto them, When ye pray, say, Our Father which art in heaven, Hallowed be thy name. Thy kingdom come. Thy will be done, as in heaven, so in earth.*

Luke 11:2”

“*But I say unto you, That every idle word that men shall speak, they shall give account thereof in the day of judgment.*

Matthew 12:36”

“*This people draweth nigh unto me with their mouth, and honoureth me with their lips; but their heart is far from me. But in vain they do worship me, teaching for doctrines the commandments of men.*

Matthew 15:8, 9”

“*And call no man your father upon the earth: for one is your Father, which is in heaven.*

Matthew 23:9”

“*Let as many servants as are under the yoke count their own masters worthy of all honour, that the name of God and his doctrine be not blasphemed.*

1 Timothy 6:1”

The Vedas

We read in the Holy Bible that God calls His name as "I Am", as seen in ***Isaiah 42:8***, above. Sai Baba has spoken of this 'I am' as the divine sweetness that pervades everything in the Universe, being the unchanging substratum that underlies all the changing names and forms. It is the 'I' that makes up God's shining existence and presence in all Creation; "I am the Self in the heart of all beings".

> "*I am the beginning, the middle, and the end.*
> ***Rig Veda, Purusha Sukta***"

> "*Every time we say 'I' or 'I am' we are confirming that God exists; what's more, it proclaims that He exists in us, for that is what we call ourselves. To say, "I am just a wretched sinner, a lowly, unimportant nobody", has to be a falsehood and therefore is taking the name of the Lord in vain. Here then is the deeper essence meaning of this commandment. "Say, 'I am a child of immortality' or 'I am the embodiment of love and peace and bliss.' And not only say so, but live your life accordingly." says Baba. That is the way to glorify the Name. "Let your life be your message, just as my life is my message. Live in love, Live in God, for truly that you are.*
> ***Sai Baba, Shirdi***"

Conclusion

As seen in the Holy Scriptures, the Name of God is the Greatest, the Holiest and Matchless. The Name of God is not to be used for vain promises and for wrong uses (*God-Promise; for God's sake; on God; swear on God* etc.). It can be noticed here that when a couple is in a relationship of love, they tend to defend each other, whatsoever. Similarly, this Commandment encourages us to develop such binding relationship with our Maker - God.

> "*Behold, a virgin shall be with child, and shall bring forth a son, and they shall call his name Emmanuel, which being interpreted is, God with us.*
> ***Matthew 1:23***"

Jesus has been named as **Emmanuel**. The name means **God with us**! This shows the Almighty God's close presence with us.

On the other hand, in our earthy lives, we care so much for our names. We make sure that we do not commit crime or do not do any foolish things which may hamper our reputation or the name of the family. We often hear parents telling their children to fare well in their exams to keep the family name and maintain the legacy. How much more, being children of the Almighty God, is it necessary for us to see that His Name is not tarnished by our foolish acts, including vocabulary, ways of life, food we eat, addictions etc.?

The Third Commandment calls us to be sober, vigilant, loving, patient, good, kind, gentle and encourages to acquire the qualities of the Character of God. Imagine, how beautiful this earth would be with people filled with love, compassion and goodness. God would literally dwell among us!

CHAPTER EIGHTEEN

The Fourth Commandment

Seventh day Sabbath

The Holy Bible

> "*Remember the sabbath day, to keep it holy. Six days shalt thou labour, and do all thy work: But the seventh day is the sabbath of the LORD thy God: in it thou shalt not do any work, thou, nor thy son, nor thy daughter, thy manservant, nor thy maidservant, nor thy cattle, nor thy stranger that is within thy gates: For in six days the LORD made heaven and earth, the sea, and all that in them is, and rested the seventh day: wherefore the LORD blessed the sabbath day, and hallowed it.*
>
> ***Exodus 20:8 - 11***"

> "*Keep the sabbath day to sanctify it, as the LORD thy God hath commanded thee. Six days thou shalt labour, and do all thy work: But the seventh day is the sabbath of the LORD thy God: in it thou shalt not do any work, thou, nor thy son,*

nor thy daughter, nor thy manservant, nor thy maidservant, nor thine ox, nor thine ass, nor any of thy cattle, nor thy stranger that is within thy gates; that thy manservant and thy maidservant may rest as well as thou. And remember that thou wast a servant in the land of Egypt, and that the LORD thy God brought thee out thence through a mighty hand and by a stretched out arm: therefore the LORD thy God commanded thee to keep the sabbath day.

Deuteronomy 5:12 - 15"

"*And it came to pass, that on the sixth day they gathered twice as much bread, two omers for one man: and all the rulers of the congregation came and told Moses. And he said unto them, This is that which the LORD hath said, To morrow is the rest of the holy sabbath unto the LORD: bake that which ye will bake to day, and seethe that ye will seethe; and that which remaineth over lay up for you to be kept until the morning. And they laid it up till the morning, as Moses bade: and it did not stink, neither was there any worm therein. And Moses said, Eat that to day; for to day is a sabbath unto the LORD: to day ye shall not find it in the field. Six days ye shall gather it; but on the seventh day, which is the sabbath, in it there shall be none. And it came to pass, that there went out some of the people on the seventh day for to gather, and they found none. And the LORD said unto Moses, How long refuse ye to keep my commandments and my laws? See, for that the LORD hath given you the sabbath, therefore he giveth you on the sixth day the bread of two days; abide ye every man in his place, let no man go out of his place on the seventh day. So the people rested on the seventh day.*

Exodus 16:23 - 30"

"*And the LORD spake unto Moses, saying, Speak thou also unto the children of Israel, saying, Verily my sabbaths ye shall keep: for it is a sign between me and you throughout your generations; that ye may know that I am the LORD that doth sanctify you. Ye shall keep the sabbath therefore; for it is holy unto you: every one that defileth it shall surely be put to death: for whosoever doeth any work therein, that soul shall be cut off from among his people. Six days may work be done; but in the seventh is the sabbath of rest, holy to the LORD: whosoever doeth any work in the sabbath day, he shall surely be put to death. Wherefore the children of Israel shall keep the sabbath, to observe the sabbath throughout their generations, for a perpetual covenant. It is a sign between me and the children of Israel for ever: for in six days the LORD made heaven and earth, and on the seventh day he rested, and was refreshed.*

Exodus 31:12 - 17"

"*Six days thou shalt do thy work, and on the seventh day thou shalt rest: that thine ox and thine ass may rest, and the son of thy handmaid, and the stranger, may be refreshed.*

Exodus 23:12"

"*Six days thou shalt work, but on the seventh day thou shalt rest: in earing time and in harvest thou shalt rest.*

Exodus 34:21"

"*Six days shall work be done, but on the seventh day there shall be to you an holy day, a sabbath of rest to the LORD: whosoever doeth work therein shall be put to death.*

Exodus 35:2"

"*Six days shall work be done: but the seventh day is the sabbath of rest, an holy convocation; ye shall do no work therein: it is the sabbath of the LORD in all your dwellings.*

Leviticus 23:3"

"*Thus the heavens and the earth were finished, and all the host of them. And on the seventh day God ended his work which he had made; and he rested on the seventh day from all his work which he had made. And God blessed the seventh day, and sanctified it: because that in it he had rested from all his work which God created and made.*
Genesis 2:1 - 3"

"*For the Son of man is Lord even of the sabbath day.*
Matthew 12:8"

"*And he said unto them, That the Son of man is Lord also of the sabbath.*
Luke 6:5."

So the Sabbath is the Biblical Lord's Day.

"*How much then is a man better than a sheep? Wherefore it is lawful to do well on the sabbath days.*
Matthew 12:12"

"*But pray ye that your flight be not in the winter, neither on the sabbath day:*
Matthew 24:20."

Speaking of the time of tribulation just before His second coming.

"*And they went into Capernaum; and straightway on the sabbath day he entered into the synagogue, and taught.*
Mark 1:21"

"*And he said unto them, The sabbath was made for man, and not man for the sabbath: Therefore the Son of man is Lord also of the sabbath.*
Mark 2:27, 28."

Notice: The Sabbath is **not** just for Jews, or Israelites, or Hebrews, or Semites (descendants of Shem), but **for all mankind**.

> "*And when the sabbath day was come, he began to teach in the synagogue: and many hearing him were astonished, saying, From whence hath this man these things? and what wisdom is this which is given unto him, that even such mighty works are wrought by his hands?*
> ***Mark 6:2***"

> "*And he came to Nazareth, where he had been brought up: and, as his custom was, he went into the synagogue on the sabbath day, and stood up for to read.*
> ***Luke 4:16***"

> "*And came down to Capernaum, a city of Galilee, and taught them on the sabbath days.*
> ***Luke 4:31***"

> "*And the women also, which came with him from Galilee, followed after, and beheld the sepulchre, and how his body was laid. And they returned, and prepared spices and ointments; and rested the sabbath day according to the commandment.*
> ***Luke 23:55, 56.***"

This occurred after Jesus' death, which is when the false teachers claim the law was done away. They say the law was "nailed to the cross", but His disciples obviously didn't believe that, as we see here, they "rested the Sabbath day according to the commandment" After Jesus' death, his disciples observed the sabbath.

> "*But when they departed from Perga, they came to Antioch in Pisidia, and went into the synagogue on the sabbath day, and sat down.*

Acts 13:14"

"*And when the Jews were gone out of the synagogue, the Gentiles besought that these words might be preached to them the next sabbath.*

Acts 13:42."

Notice: the Gentiles (non-Jews) wanted to hear the word of God on the next Sabbath. Paul **did not** tell them, "Come back tomorrow, the first day of the week, because that's the day us Christians keep." He had them return the following **Sabbath.**

"*And the next sabbath day came almost the whole city together to hear the word of God.*

Acts 13:44"

"*For Moses of old time hath in every city them that preach him, being read in the synagogues every sabbath day.*

Acts 15:21"

"*And on the sabbath we went out of the city by a river side, where prayer was wont to be made; and we sat down, and spake unto the women which resorted thither.*

Acts 16:13"

"*And Paul, as his manner was, went in unto them, and three sabbath days reasoned with them out of the scriptures,*

Acts 17:2"

"*And he reasoned in the synagogue every sabbath, and persuaded the Jews and the Greeks.*

Acts 18:4"

"*For he spake in a certain place of the seventh day on this wise, And God did rest the seventh day from all his works.*

Hebrews 4:4"

"*There remaineth therefore a rest to the people of God.*

Hebrews 4:9."

See margin: Greek word for **rest**, here is **Sabbatismos** which means **Sabbath-keeping.**

"*For as the new heavens and the new earth, which I will make, shall remain before me, saith the LORD, so shall your seed and your name remain. And it shall come to pass, that from one new moon to another, and from one sabbath to another, shall all flesh come to worship before me, saith the LORD.*

Isaiah 66:22, 23."

We can clearly see here, this is dealing with the **New heavens and earth** (after Christ's return) and it states that all shall keep the Sabbath then. It seems quite absurd, that God would give the seventh day Sabbath to mankind at creation **(Genesis 2:1 - 3)**, reintroduce it to Israel before Sinai - after they lost sight of it in captivity **(Exodus 16:4, 23, 27 - 29)**, codify it at Sinai **(Exodus 20)** having all His people observe it, including Christ, then change it to Sunday, just to change it back to Friday sunset - Saturday sunset. **The sabbath has never changed and is still to be observed!**

The Vedas

The Vedas specifically don't say much on the Fourth Commandment. Humanity in its sin, wanted to relate to God, every moment. Thus Vedas were revealed to the sages, in historic times, without a light over this topic.

Conclusion

As seen in the Holy Bible, Sabbath was instituted right at the Creation. It was present before Christ visited this Earth and also during His visitation. We also saw that Christ's disciples kept the Sabbath day, after His death & resurrection too. The Bible says that Sabbath will be kept in Eternity, as well.

The importance of the Sabbath is not merely observing a day - *Friday sunset to Saturday sunset* (as per the Holy Bible). It is quite more than that!

Sabbath was established by God to have a wonderful fellowship and time with Humanity. During this appointed and sanctified time, Humanity was supposed to closely behold God and continue a quality relationship with Him and then display the Character of God (Love) to all universe.

The Fourth Commandment calls us to have the complete Character of God, Who is Unconditional Love, and reflect Him to every creature in the universe. How? By beholding Him continually.

CHAPTER NINETEEN

THE FIFTH COMMANDMENT

Honour parents

The Holy Bible

"*Honour thy father and thy mother: that thy days may be long upon the land which the LORD thy God giveth thee.*
Exodus 20:12"

"*Honour thy father and thy mother, as the LORD thy God hath commanded thee; that thy days may be prolonged, and that it may go well with thee, in the land which the LORD thy God giveth thee.*
Deuteronomy 5:16"

"*Cursed be he that setteth light by his father or his mother. And all the people shall say, Amen.*
Deuteronomy 27:16"

"*For God commanded, saying, Honour thy father and mother: and, He that curseth father or mother, let him die the death.*

Matthew 15:4"

"*For Moses said, Honour thy father and thy mother; and, Whoso curseth father or mother, let him die the death:*

Mark 7:10"

"*Honour thy father and thy mother: and, Thou shalt love thy neighbour as thyself.*

Matthew 19:19"

"*Thou knowest the commandments, Do not commit adultery, Do not kill, Do not steal, Do not bear false witness, Defraud not, Honour thy father and mother.*

Mark 10:19"

"*Thou knowest the commandments, Do not commit adultery, Do not kill, Do not steal, Do not bear false witness, Honour thy father and thy mother.*

Luke 18:20"

"*And even as they did not like to retain God in their knowledge, God gave them over to a reprobate mind, to do those things which are not convenient; Being filled with all unrighteousness, fornication, wickedness, covetousness, maliciousness; full of envy, murder, debate, deceit, malignity; whisperers, Backbiters, haters of God, despiteful, proud, boasters, inventors of evil things, disobedient to parents, Without understanding, covenantbreakers, without natural affection, implacable, unmerciful: Who knowing the judgment of God, that they which commit such things are worthy of death, not only do the same, but have pleasure in them that do them.*

Romans 1:28 - 32 ”

“*Children, obey your parents in the Lord: for this is right. Honour thy father and mother; (which is the first commandment with promise;) That it may be well with thee, and thou mayest live long on the earth.*

Ephesians 6:1 - 3 ”

“*Children, obey your parents in all things: for this is well pleasing unto the Lord.*

Colossians 3:16 ”

“*But if any widow have children or nephews, let them learn first to shew piety at home, and to requite their parents: for that is good and acceptable before God.*

1 Timothy 5:4 ”

The Vedas

“*The obedience to mother, father and preceptor (teacher) is most important according to me. The man who attends to that duty here, succeeds in acquiring great fame and many regions of felicity. Obeyed with respect by thee, whatever they will command thee, be it consistent with righteousness or inconsistent with it, should be done unhesitatingly, O Yudhishthir! One should never do what they forbid. Without doubt, that which they command should always be done.*

Bheeshma, Mahabharata ”

“*Never transgress them in any act. Never eat before they eat, nor eat anything that is better than what they eat. Never impute any fault to them. One should always serve them with humility. That is an act of high merit. By acting in that way, o best of kings, you may obtain fame, merit, honour, and regions of felicity hereafter. He who honours these three is honoured in all the worlds. He, on the other hand, who disregards these three, fails to obtain any merit from any of his acts.*

***Mahabharata, Shanti Parva, Section 108*"**

Conclusion

As seen, both in the Holy Bible and the Vedas, God considers it very important to honour and obey parents. It pleases God to see that children obey their parents.

This also reminds us that **God Himself is ourParent** and we need to obey Him in all ways. It is His Love for us that He gave us this Commandment. He always desires good for us and wants us to be safe and sound, now and for eternity to come. His choices and will for us are never harmful. They are always the best. How wonderful is it to have the Creator, the Almighty God as our own Parent.

The Fifth Commandment, hence calls us to obey Him as our Parent. This commandment reveals to us His Character as our very own Parent, to Whom we can open ourselves completely, without fear.

This Commandment shows us the importance of our parents in our lives, their role in bringing us to life, their love & sacrifice, which reflect us the Love of God, His role as our Creator, the One Who Himself is Life and has given us Life, His sacrifice to save us - God is marvellous!

In the sweet parent-children relationship, God shows us how close He is to us. Our very own Parent.

CHAPTER TWENTY

THE SIXTH COMMANDMENT

Murder

The Holy Bible

"*Thou shalt not kill.*
Exodus 20:13"

"*Thou shalt not kill.*
Deuteronomy 5:17"

"*Whoso sheddeth man's blood, by man shall his blood be shed: for in the image of God made he man.*
Genesis 9:6"

"*And he that killeth any man shall surely be put to death.*
Leviticus 24:17"

"*Ye have heard that it was said by them of old time, Thou shalt not kill; and whosoever shall kill shall be in danger of the judgment: But I say unto you, That whosoever is angry with his brother without a cause shall be in danger of the judgment: and whosoever shall say to his brother, Raca, shall be in danger of the council: but whosoever shall say, Thou fool, shall be in danger of hell fire.*

Matthew 5:21, 22"

"*He that saith he is in the light, and hateth his brother, is in darkness even until now.*

1 John 2:9. *In light of* ***Matthew 5:21, 22***."

"*And he said unto him, Why callest thou me good? there is none good but one, that is, God: but if thou wilt enter into life, keep the commandments. He saith unto him, Which? Jesus said, Thou shalt do no murder, Thou shalt not commit adultery, Thou shalt not steal, Thou shalt not bear false witness, Honour thy father and thy mother: and, Thou shalt love thy neighbour as thyself.*

Matthew 19:17 - 19"

"*Thou knowest the commandments, Do not commit adultery, Do not kill, Do not steal, Do not bear false witness, Defraud not, Honour thy father and mother.*

Mark 10:19"

"*Thou knowest the commandments, Do not commit adultery, Do not kill, Do not steal, Do not bear false witness, Honour thy father and thy mother.*

Luke 18:20"

"*For this, Thou shalt not commit adultery, Thou shalt not kill, Thou shalt not steal, Thou shalt not bear false witness, Thou shalt not covet; and if there be any other commandment, it is briefly comprehended in this saying, namely, Thou shalt love thy neighbour as thyself.*

Romans 13:9"

"*For he that said, Do not commit adultery, said also, Do not kill. Now if thou commit no adultery, yet if thou kill, thou art become a transgressor of the law.*

James 2:11"

"*But let none of you suffer as a murderer, or as a thief, or as an evildoer, or as a busybody in other men's matters.*

1 Peter 4:15"

"*We know that we have passed from death unto life, because we love the brethren. He that loveth not his brother abideth in death. Whosoever hateth his brother is a murderer: and ye know that no murderer hath eternal life abiding in him.*

1 John 3:14, 15"

The Vedas

"*You must not use your God-given body for killing God's creatures, whether they are human, animal or whatever.*

Yajur Veda 12:32"

"*By not killing any living being, one becomes eligible for salvation.*

Manusmriti 6:60"

"*Ahimsa (nonviolence) is the highest duty.*

Padma Purana 1:31:27"

Conclusion

As seen from the verses above, both the Holy Bible and the Vedas strictly forbid killing. The Holy Bible goes further to say that even anger from no reason is equal to murder.

This Commandment shows us a very **sweet part** of the Nature of God - **Forgiving** & **Love**. This shows us that God is not interested in manslaughter or killing animals or any living beings to satisfy Himself. His Nature, tells us that He wants us to have abundance of Life, as **He Himself is Life**. His Love for us is that He is ready to forgive us whenever we ask Him to forgive us. In fact, in the death of His Son, God already forgave us. This is solely because God Himself died for our transgressions. The Vedas predicted this in the **sacrificial death of Purusha, the Almighty**. The Holy Bible records both - the prophecy and its fulfilment in the **sacrificial death of Jesus Christ**, on behalf of humanity.

The Sixth Commandment, thus calls us to have a pure and wonderful character of love, which symbolizes the Love of God for us. He has thus granted us wonderful relationships of parents, siblings, friends and pets, in whom we can exercise this wonderful Character of God - Love.

CHAPTER TWENTY-ONE

THE SEVENTH COMMANDMENT

Adultery

The Holy Bible

> "*Thou shalt not commit adultery.*
> **_Exodus 20:14_**"

> "*Neither shalt thou commit adultery.*
> **_Deuteronomy 5:18_**"

> "*And the man that committeth adultery with another man's wife, even he that committeth adultery with his neighbour's wife, the adulterer and the adulteress shall surely be put to death.*
> **_Leviticus 20:10_**"

> "*Ye have heard that it was said by them of old time, Thou shalt not commit adultery: But I say unto you, That whosoever looketh on a woman to lust after her hath*

committed adultery with her already in his heart.

Matthew 5:27, 28. *Lustful fantasies, masturbation etc., are equal to adultery.*"

"*But I say unto you, That whosoever shall put away his wife, saving for the cause of fornication, causeth her to commit adultery: and whosoever shall marry her that is divorced committeth adultery.*

Matthew 5:32"

"*And he said unto him, Why callest thou me good? there is none good but one, that is, God: but if thou wilt enter into life, keep the commandments. He saith unto him, Which? Jesus said, Thou shalt do no murder, Thou shalt not commit adultery, Thou shalt not steal, Thou shalt not bear false witness, Honour thy father and thy mother: and, Thou shalt love thy neighbour as thyself.*

Matthew 19:17 - 19"

"*Thou knowest the commandments, Do not commit adultery, Do not kill, Do not steal, Do not bear false witness, Defraud not, Honour thy father and mother.*

Mark 10:19"

"*Thou knowest the commandments, Do not commit adultery, Do not kill, Do not steal, Do not bear false witness, Honour thy father and thy mother.*

Luke 18:20"

"*And he saith unto them, Whosoever shall put away his wife, and marry another, committeth adultery against her. And if a woman shall put away her husband, and be married to another, she committeth adultery.*

Mark 10:11, 12"

"*Whosoever putteth away his wife, and marrieth another, committeth adultery: and whosoever marrieth her that is put away from her husband committeth adultery.*

Luke 16:18"

"*They say unto him, Master, this woman was taken in adultery, in the very act. Now Moses in the law commanded us, that such should be stoned: but what sayest thou? This they said, tempting him, that they might have to accuse him. But Jesus stooped down, and with his finger wrote on the ground, as though he heard them not. So when they continued asking him, he lifted up himself, and said unto them, He that is without sin among you, let him first cast a stone at her. And again he stooped down, and wrote on the ground. And they which heard it, being convicted by their own conscience, went out one by one, beginning at the eldest, even unto the last: and Jesus was left alone, and the woman standing in the midst. When Jesus had lifted up himself, and saw none but the woman, he said unto her, Woman, where are those thine accusers? hath no man condemned thee? She said, No man, Lord. And Jesus said unto her, Neither do I condemn thee: go, and sin no more.*

John 8:4 - 11"

"*So then if, while her husband liveth, she be married to another man, she shall be called an adulteress: but if her husband be dead, she is free from that law; so that she is no adulteress, though she be married to another man.*

Romans 7:3"

"*For this, Thou shalt not commit adultery, Thou shalt not kill, Thou shalt not steal, Thou shalt not bear false witness, Thou shalt not covet; and if there be any other commandment, it is briefly comprehended in this saying, namely, Thou shalt love thy neighbour as thyself.*

Romans 13:9 "

"*Know ye not that the unrighteous shall not inherit the kingdom of God? Be not deceived: neither fornicators, nor idolaters, nor adulterers, nor effeminate, nor abusers of themselves with mankind, Nor thieves, nor covetous, nor drunkards, nor revilers, nor extortioners, shall inherit the kingdom of God.*

1 Corinthians 6:9, 10 "

"*Flee fornication. Every sin that a man doeth is without the body; but he that committeth fornication sinneth against his own body.*

1 Corinthians 6:18 "

"*Now the works of the flesh are manifest, which are these; Adultery, fornication, uncleanness, lasciviousness, Idolatry, witchcraft, hatred, variance, emulations, wrath, strife, seditions, heresies, Envyings, murders, drunkenness, revellings, and such like: of the which I tell you before, as I have also told you in time past, that they which do such things shall not inherit the kingdom of God.*

Galatians 5:19 - 21 "

"*For this is the will of God, even your sanctification, that ye should abstain from fornication:*

1 Thessalonians 4:3 "

"*Marriage is honourable in all, and the bed undefiled: but whoremongers and adulterers God will judge.*

Hebrews 13:4 "

"*For he that said, Do not commit adultery, said also, Do not kill. Now if thou commit no adultery, yet if thou kill, thou art become a transgressor of the law.*

James 2:11"

"*Even as Sodom and Gomorrha, and the cities about them in like manner, giving themselves over to fornication, and going after strange flesh, are set forth for an example, suffering the vengeance of eternal fire.*

Jude 1:7"

"*And I gave her space to repent of her fornication; and she repented not. Behold, I will cast her into a bed, and them that commit adultery with her into great tribulation, except they repent of their deeds.*

Revelation 2:21, 22"

The Vedas

The Vedas is unusually very silent on this matter of adultery. Ancient sages never understood this as sin and hence they never prayed for light on this matter. But, when the fruits of this sin was slowly witnessed, wherein marriages were defiled by extramarital relationships, many leaders stepped forward to bring forth their views on adultery. Some are listed.

"*A man should not think incontinently of another's wife, much less address her to that end; for such a man will is doomed. A man who commits adultery is punished both here and hereafter; for his days in this world are cut short, and when dead he falls into hell.*

Vishnu Purana 3:11."

This verse was added to Vishnu Purana at a very later stage.

"*A man formerly accused of such offences (adultery), who secretly converses with another man's wife, shall pay the first*

fine. He who addresses the wife of another man at a tirtha, outside the village, in a forest, or at the confluence of rivers, suffer the punishment for adulterous acts.
Manusmriti 8:354, 356"

"*Women must particularly be guarded against evil inclinations, however trifling they may appear; for, if they are not guarded, they will bring sorrow on two families.*
Manusmriti 9:5"

Conclusion

As seen clearly from the Holy Bible, **marriage is a pure unity, ordained by God Himself**. Any physical or mental relationship outside marriage is defilement of one's character, being guilty of adultery.

The Seventh Commandment, thus calls us to be pure and holy in thoughts, just as our Almighty God is - Pure, Holy & Undefiled. This Commandment shows God's Purity to us and reveals the dirt and filthiness within ourselves, encouraging us to be perfect in our ways.

Also, this Commandment reveals to us that God is the One, in Whom we have our being. He is the reason for our existence. He is the Only One worthy to receive our worship. Thus, worshipping other gods, as seen in the First Commandment becomes a sort of adultery! Even ***Bhagvad Gita 7:22*** says that other demigods have no power, as they are imaginations of humans, thus resulting in adultery among men! We see here a close connection between the First, Second & the Seventh Commandments.

CHAPTER TWENTY-TWO

THE EIGHT COMMANDMENT

Theft

The Holy Bible

"*Thou shalt not steal.*
Exodus 20:15"

"*Neither shalt thou steal.*
Deuteronomy 5:19"

"*Ye shall not steal, neither deal falsely, neither lie one to another.*
Leviticus 5:19"

"*And he said unto him, Why callest thou me good? there is none good but one, that is, God: but if thou wilt enter into life, keep the commandments. He saith unto him, Which? Jesus said, Thou shalt do no murder, Thou shalt not commit adultery, Thou shalt not steal, Thou shalt not bear false witness, Honour thy father and thy mother: and, Thou shalt love thy neighbour as thyself.*

Matthew 19:17 - 19"

"*Thou knowest the commandments, Do not commit adultery, Do not kill, Do not steal, Do not bear false witness, Defraud not, Honour thy father and mother.*

Mark 10:19"

"*Thou knowest the commandments, Do not commit adultery, Do not kill, Do not steal, Do not bear false witness, Honour thy father and thy mother.*

Luke 18:20"

"*For this, Thou shalt not commit adultery, Thou shalt not kill, Thou shalt not steal, Thou shalt not bear false witness, Thou shalt not covet; and if there be any other commandment, it is briefly comprehended in this saying, namely, Thou shalt love thy neighbour as thyself.*

Romans 13:9"

"*Know ye not that the unrighteous shall not inherit the kingdom of God? Be not deceived: neither fornicators, nor idolaters, nor adulterers, nor effeminate, nor abusers of themselves with mankind, Nor thieves, nor covetous, nor drunkards, nor revilers, nor extortioners, shall inherit the kingdom of God.*

1 Corinthians 6:9, 10"

"*Let him that stole steal no more: but rather let him labour, working with his hands the thing which is good, that he may have to give to him that needeth.*

Ephesians 4:28"

"*But let none of you suffer as a murderer, or as a thief, or as an evildoer, or as a busybody in other men's matters.*
1 Peter 4:15"

"*Neither repented they of their murders, nor of their sorceries, nor of their fornication, nor of their thefts.*
Revelation 9:21"

The Vedas

"*Do not covet the wealth of others. Evidently stealing is very mean act. Therefore, man should abstain from stealing.*
Yajur Veda 40:1"

Conclusion

We see from the verses above that stealing has been termed a sinful act. Though the entire Vedas give us only one verse on stealing, it speaks against it. The Holy Bible speaks against stealing, defining it to be an act of sin, leading to eternal destruction.

Stealing is an act which makes us to claim something which is not ours! It has its roots in falsehood! God strictly tells us to abstain from such acts.

The Eighth Commandment, thus calls us to be noble, virtuous & hardworking and encourages us to run away from stealing, falsehood & injustice. This shows us the Pure, Sublime and Holy Character of God. When He claims something, He really means it, as everything is owned by Him - the whole Universe.

You, all living beings and I, are owned by the Almighty God. This Commandment redirects us into His Ownership, telling us to stop stealing our own selves from Him by doing our own pleasures and harming ourselves! God knows the best for us. This Commandment calls us for obeying Him, Who is our Owner and our very own - God, our Owner.

CHAPTER TWENTY-THREE

The Ninth Commandment

Lying

The Holy Bible

"*Thou shalt not bear false witness against thy neighbour.*
Exodus 20:16"

"*Neither shalt thou bear false witness against thy neighbour.*
Deuteronomy 5:20"

"*Thou shalt not raise a false report: put not thine hand with the wicked to be an unrighteous witness.*
Exodus 23:1"

"*But I say unto you, That every idle word that men shall speak, they shall give account thereof in the day of judgment. For by thy words thou shalt be justified, and by thy words thou shalt be condemned.*

Matthew 12:36, 37"

"*For out of the heart proceed evil thoughts, murders, adulteries, fornications, thefts, false witness, blasphemies: These are the things which defile a man: but to eat with unwashen hands defileth not a man.*

Matthew 15:19, 20"

"*And he said unto him, Why callest thou me good? there is none good but one, that is, God: but if thou wilt enter into life, keep the commandments. He saith unto him, Which? Jesus said, Thou shalt do no murder, Thou shalt not commit adultery, Thou shalt not steal, Thou shalt not bear false witness, Honour thy father and thy mother: and, Thou shalt love thy neighbour as thyself.*

Matthew 19:17 - 19"

"*Thou knowest the commandments, Do not commit adultery, Do not kill, Do not steal, Do not bear false witness, Defraud not, Honour thy father and mother.*

Mark 10:19"

"*Thou knowest the commandments, Do not commit adultery, Do not kill, Do not steal, Do not bear false witness, Honour thy father and thy mother.*

Luke 18:20"

"*For this, Thou shalt not commit adultery, Thou shalt not kill, Thou shalt not steal, Thou shalt not bear false witness, Thou shalt not covet; and if there be any other commandment, it is briefly comprehended in this saying, namely, Thou shalt love thy neighbour as thyself.*

Romans 13:9"

"*Ye are of your father the devil, and the lusts of your father ye will do. He was a murderer from the beginning, and abode not in the truth, because there is no truth in him. When he speaketh a lie, he speaketh of his own: for he is a liar, and the father of it.*

John 8:44"

"*But have renounced the hidden things of dishonesty, not walking in craftiness, nor handling the word of God deceitfully; but by manifestation of the truth commending ourselves to every man's conscience in the sight of God.*

2 Corinthians 4:2"

"*Wherefore putting away lying, speak every man truth with his neighbour: for we are members one of another.*

Ephesians 4:25"

"*Lie not one to another, seeing that ye have put off the old man with his deeds;*

Colossians 3:9"

"*Even so must their wives be grave, not slanderers, sober, faithful in all things.*

1 Timothy 3:11"

"*To speak evil of no man, to be no brawlers, but gentle, shewing all meekness unto all men.*

Titus 3:2"

"*But the fearful, and unbelieving, and the abominable, and murderers, and whoremongers, and sorcerers, and idolaters, and all liars, shall have their part in the lake which burneth with fire and brimstone: which is the second death.*

Revelation 21:8"

"*For without are dogs, and sorcerers, and whoremongers, and murderers, and idolaters, and whosoever loveth and maketh a lie.*

Revelation 22:15"

The Vedas

"*Who is not to be trusted?' The answer is 'one who as a rule utters lies'.*

Adi Shankaracharya, Prashna Uttara Ratna Malika 46"

"*Pandav Yudhishthir always spoke the truth. He was honoured for his stand for the truth.*

Mahabharata"

Conclusion

We see clearly that both, the Vedas and the Holy Bible tell us to always speak the truth. This teaches us of a very vital part of the Character of God - **Truth**. He can never lie, because the other name of Truth is God Almighty.

We thus read in the Holy Bible, in ***John 14:6***, where Jesus says,

"*"I am the Truth..."*"

This shows us the Purity of God's Character. Whatever He has promised, He will definitely fulfil it, because He spoke the Truth. It is His essence.

"Truth always triumphs" is an English proverb, also available in other languages. Truth - the word itself explains purity, sublimity, authenticity and no guile present in it!

The Ninth Commandment calls us to experience God in truth. His Love is the Truth. His existence is the Truth. He brought forth everything into existence - the living truth. Our very existence shows the Truth of God. Truth is a reflection of God's Pure, Sublime, Authentic, Holy & Matchless Character.

CHAPTER TWENTY-FOUR

The Tenth Commandment

Covetousness and Lust

The Holy Bible

> "*Thou shalt not covet thy neighbour's house, thou shalt not covet thy neighbour's wife, nor his manservant, nor his maidservant, nor his ox, nor his ass, nor any thing that is thy neighbour's.*
>
> **Exodus 20:17**"

> "*Neither shalt thou desire thy neighbour's wife, neither shalt thou covet thy neighbour's house, his field, or his manservant, or his maidservant, his ox, or his ass, or any thing that is thy neighbour's.*
>
> **Deuteronomy 5:21**"

> "*And he said unto them, Take heed, and beware of covetousness: for a man's life consisteth not in the abundance of the things which he possesseth.*

Luke 12:15"

"*What shall we say then? Is the law sin? God forbid. Nay, I had not known sin, but by the law: for I had not known lust, except the law had said, Thou shalt not covet.*

Romans 7:7"

"*For this, Thou shalt not commit adultery, Thou shalt not kill, Thou shalt not steal, Thou shalt not bear false witness, Thou shalt not covet; and if there be any other commandment, it is briefly comprehended in this saying, namely, Thou shalt love thy neighbour as thyself.*

Romans 13:9"

"*But fornication, and all uncleanness, or covetousness, let it not be once named among you, as becometh saints;*

Ephesians 5:3"

"*For the love of money is the root of all evil: which while some coveted after, they have erred from the faith, and pierced themselves through with many sorrows.*

1 Timothy 6:10"

"*Let your conversation be without covetousness; and be content with such things as ye have: for he hath said, I will never leave thee, nor forsake thee.*

Hebrews 13:5"

The Vedas

"*Destroy all those who are lustful, angry, greedy, enticed, proud and jealous.*

Atharva Veda"

"*The hypocritical and the greedy are struck down the Messenger of Death punishes them with his club*
Atharva Veda"

"*Do not covet the wealth of others. Evidently stealing is very mean act. Therefore, man should abstain from stealing.*
Yajur Veda 40:1"

Conclusion

As seen in the verses above, a greedy man is destined to destruction. The Holy Bible & the Vedas instruct us not to be covetous or greedy.

The Tenth Commandment calls us not to be covetous and greedy. It tells us to be Selfless and simple. This Commandment shows us the **Selflessness in God's Character**. When we see Him creating everything and then dying for us to save us, we see His Selfless Love, by which He gave Himself for us. God is Love. Selfless Love! Agape!

CHAPTER TWENTY-FIVE

THE PERFECT UNDERSTANDING

We learnt from above, the Ten Commandments are a reflection of God's Character. Jesus summed the whole of the Ten Commandments into two simple ones:

> "*Jesus said unto him, Thou shalt love the Lord thy God with all thy heart, and with all thy soul, and with all thy mind. This is the first and great commandment. And the second is like unto it, Thou shalt love thy neighbour as thyself. On these two commandments hang all the law and the prophets.*
> ***Matthew 22:37 - 40***"

Love is the essence of the Character of God.

Love God - this fulfils the first four Commandments. When we love God with all of our heart, soul and mind, we cannot think of any other gods before Him, or can't make any image of Him or love something else more than Him. We care the utmost for His Name and tend to look forward to spend a quality time with Him, during His appointed Day - the Sabbath.

Love your Neighbour - this fulfils the next six Commandments. When we love our fellowmen, we respect them (including our parents) and can't kill them or cheat them, immorally. We can't think of stealing from or lie to them as they are the objects of our love. Our greed hence finds no place in our heart!

Hence, we can sum up the Ten Commandments, in understanding God, as follows:

- 1st Commandment: ***God is Almighty.*** There is none like Him.
- 2nd Commandment: ***God is the Creator.*** He cannot be created. Nothing stands before Him.
- 3rd Commandment: ***God is Righteousness.*** His Name shows His Might. Emmanuel, God with us.
- 4th Commandment: ***God is Love.*** Beholding Him changes us, completely.
- 5th Commandment: ***God is our Parent.*** He is very close to us. He is Trustworthy.
- 6th Commandment: ***God is Life.***
- 7th Commandment: ***God is Pure, Holy and Undefiled.***
- 8th Commandment: ***God is our Owner.***
- 9th Commandment: ***God is the Truth.***
- 10th Commandment: ***God is Selfless.***

Printed by Libri Plureos GmbH in Hamburg,
Germany